To Joel, Benjamin, Chloe, and Jeremy
—*From Grandpa, with love*

Photo credits: Cover, © Dr. Alan K. Mallams; Endpapers (front), p. 2, ©
Dr. Alan K. Mallams, p. 3. © 1998 Scott Barrow; Title page, © Dr. Alan K.
Mallams; p. 6, © Dr. Alan K. Mallams; p. 9, © Dr. Alan K. Mallams; p. 11, ©
Dr. Alan K. Mallams; p. 13, © 1990 Scott Barrow; p. 14, © 1993 Gary J.
Benson; p. 17, © 1993 Gary J. Benson; p. 18, © 1992 Dean Abramson; p.
21, © 1998 Scott Barrow; p. 22, © 1993 Scott Barrow; p. 25, © Dean
Abramson; p. 26, © 1992 Gary J. Benson; p. 29, © 1980 Scott Barrow; p.
30, © 1997 Scott Barrow; p. 33, © 1997 Scott Barrow; p. 34, © 1991 Gary
J. Benson; p. 37, © Dr. Alan K. Mallams; Endpapers (back), © 1997 Scott
Barrow and © 1998 Scott Barrow

Seymour Simon's Book of Trains
Copyright © 2002 by Seymour Simon
Manufactured in China by South China Printing Company Ltd.
All rights reserved.
www.harperchildrens.com

Library of Congress Cataloging-in-Publication Data
Simon, Seymour.
    Seymour Simon's book of trains / by Seymour Simon
        p.    cm.
    ISBN 0-06-028475-7 — ISBN 0-06-028476-5 (lib. bdg.)
    ISBN 0-06-446223-4 (pbk.)
    1. Railroads—Juvenile literature. [1. Railroads—Trains.] I. Title.
TF148.S55 2002                                          2001024020
385—dc21                                                       CIP
                                                                AC

Typography by Al Cetta
❖

# Seymour Simon's Book of
# TRAINS

HARPERCOLLINSPUBLISHERS

**Trains** made the world a different place. Before the invention of the train, long journeys took many weeks or months on foot or wagon. Trains changed all that. They can carry people and heavy loads over long distances in a day or two. About two hundred years ago, people and then horses were used to pull the trains. Then the steam locomotive was invented, first in England and a year later in the United States. This early-American steam locomotive has a "cowcatcher," a strong metal grill used for pushing animals or trees off the tracks.

# STEAM LOCOMOTIVES

Steam locomotives have pulled freight and passenger trains all over the world. Trains are connected cars that run along tracks called railroads. The first railroad to link the United States from coast to coast was finished in 1869. It brought the country together in a way that had never been possible before.

Here's how a steam locomotive works: Wood or coal is burned in a firebox. The heat from the fire changes water in a boiler into steam. The pressure of the steam moves pistons back and forth. As the pistons move, the wheels of the locomotive begin to turn. The engine gives off fiery sparks and clouds of smoke through a large chimney. Whistles blow and bells clang as the mighty machine chugs along the track.

# DIESEL LOCOMOTIVES

In the 1950s, diesel locomotives began replacing steam locomotives on most railroads in the United States and around the world. Diesels are faster, more powerful, and easier to fuel than steam engines. The diesel engine in a locomotive is very much like the one in a big semitrailer truck. Diesel oil is burned inside cylinders. The pistons slide back and forth and generate electric power. The electric power turns the drive wheels, and the train moves.

Several diesel locomotives supply the electric power needed to pull long trains.

# ELECTRIC TRAINS

Electric trains don't make their own power the way steam and diesel engines do. Electric trains get electric power from a third rail alongside the track or from a special overhead cable. The power comes from an electric power plant that may be a long distance away.

Electric trains are very quiet. They also don't make smoke or give off bad-smelling exhaust gases. For this reason, underground trains or subways and commuter trains that run in and around cities and their suburbs are usually electric.

# Passenger Trains

Passenger trains carry people on short or long trips. Coaches are the most commonly found cars on all kinds of passenger trains. Most coaches have rows of seats on each side of the car separated by a center aisle. Short-distance trains, such as subways and commuter trains, carry as many passengers as possible in each car.

Long-distance trains are either electric or diesel. They have more comfortable seats, toilets, and restaurant cars, as well as observation cars so that passengers can enjoy the scenery. Some long-distance trains have sleeping cars with beds so that passengers can rest at night.

# HIGH-SPEED TRAINS

High-speed trains are specially built to travel at speeds of 100 to 300 miles an hour. Bullet trains, high-speed, pointed-nose electric trains, were first put into service in Japan in 1964. New bullet trains can travel 160 miles an hour on special tracks.

The TGV, France's high-speed train, is even faster. The TGV runs along high-speed tracks between 200 and 300 miles per hour, twice as fast as a racing car. The Eurostar is a high-speed train that carries passengers from England to France or Belgium through the Chunnel, a tunnel under the English Channel.

In the United States, high-speed electric trains can travel on regular tracks between Washington, New York, and Boston.

# MOUNTAIN TRAINS

Mountain trains are sometimes called rack or cog railroad trains. They carry passengers up and down the sides of steep mountains. Rack railroads have special toothed tracks. Under its engine, the locomotive has a cogwheel with gears that fit into the teeth on the track. This allows the train to climb at very steep angles and prevents it from slipping backward down the mountainside. Mountain trains provide a safe way to view the scenery from the top of a mountain.

# FREIGHT TRAINS AND FREIGHT YARDS

Almost every day of the year, hundreds of freight trains with 60 or 70, and sometimes even as many as 200 cars, are on the move across the United States. They are pulled and pushed by several diesel locomotives. Some of the cars may be headed for one city, some for another, and still others for places in between.

The trains stop in computerized freight yards on their way to their destinations. Freight yards are full of tracks and trains. A train pulls into a receiving area. Little switcher locomotives separate and sort out the cars. They move the cars around the yard and attach them to other locomotives. Then the newly arranged trains leave for the next stops on their journeys.

# Boxcars

Boxcars look like giant shoe boxes on wheels. They have at least one sliding door on each side of the car, through which cargo is loaded and unloaded. Boxcars used to be made of wood, but now they are built of steel.

Boxcars are the most common cars on freight trains. They carry all kinds of freight, from boxes of televisions and computers to boxes of canned foods and clothing—any items that need to be protected from rain, snow, or other bad weather.

# GONDOLAS

Gondolas look like boxcars, but they do not have sliding doors on their sides. Some gondolas have roofs. Others are not covered. Some gondolas have ends with hinges or sides that can be raised or lowered for loading and unloading cargo. Other gondolas can be tilted over on their sides by special machines so that the cargo slides out easily.

Gondolas can carry heavy loads, such as building materials like concrete blocks and bricks, pipes and other plumbing supplies, machinery and wood chips.

# FLATCARS

Flatcars are open metal or wooden platforms on train wheels. They carry big items such as heavy machinery, boats, and heavy logs. Strong chains hold the cargo securely onto the platform. Sometimes wooden or metal posts line the sides and ends of flatcars for extra support.

Some flatcars are designed with sunken centers. Cranes and other tall construction machines are placed in the sunken center of the flatcar, sitting low enough so that trains can move under bridges and go through tunnels. Piggyback flatcars carry fully loaded truck trailers across the country. When the trailers arrive at their destinations, they are attached to trucks that will deliver the cargo locally on roads. Some piggyback flatcars also carry the trucks and their drivers.

# HOPPER CARS

A hopper car looks like a boxcar that has a big opening in the roof. It carries loose loads such as grain, coal, gravel, or sand. The loads are dumped or poured into the top of the car. The cargo is unloaded from chutes attached to the bottom of the hopper car.

Hopper cars have high ends and sides that prevent the cargo from spilling. The ends slant in sharply toward the middle to help the cargo fall out of the bottom chute more easily. Hopper cars that carry grain are covered for protection against the weather. Hopper cars that carry coal or gravel are open topped.

# Tank Cars

Tank cars are big steel tanks on wheels. They carry all kind of liquids, including oil, gasoline, tar, vegetable oil, milk, orange juice, and corn syrup. Some cars have more than one tank.

There are over one hundred different kinds of tank cars. Milk tank cars are built with a special clean lining made of glass or stainless steel. The lining keeps milk cool. Other tank cars have heating pipes that prevent heavy liquids, such as tar and oil, from cooling off, solidifying, and sticking to the car.

# Auto-Rack Cars

Auto-rack cars carry automobiles or trucks from the factories where they are made to places around the country where they will be sold. Auto-rack cars have two or three levels. A three-level auto rack can hold as many as eighteen automobiles.

The automobiles are driven up and down metal ramps as they are loaded and unloaded. They are tightly fastened in place so that they won't roll off while the train is moving. This auto-rack car is covered to protect the automobiles from bad weather and from getting scratched.

# Caboose

There used to be a caboose car at the end of every freight train. It was like a little house on wheels. It had bunks where the conductor and the train crew would sleep, a stove for keeping warm and cooking food, and lockers for storing tools and supplies. A telephone linked the conductor in the caboose to the engineer at the front of the train in the locomotive. The conductor was responsible for checking the freight and making sure the cargo was delivered to the correct destination. Today, computers are responsible for scheduling and running trains. Cabooses, like steam locomotives, are a reminder of past railroading times.

Day and night, trains are on the move carrying people and freight from one place to another. Trains bring fresh produce from farms and manufactured goods from factories to customers. Trains carry passengers back and forth from small towns, suburbs, and the countryside to big cities. Trains link countries from north to south and east to west. Before there were cars and planes, trains brought people together. Trains may look different now. They are run differently. But trains still bring people together.